D1242933

How Irish Immigrants Made America Home

How Irish Immigrants Made America Home

SEAN HEATHER K. MCGRAW

rosen publishing's
rosen central®

New York

Published in 2019 by The Rosen Publishing Group, Inc.
29 East 21st Street, New York, NY 10010

Copyright © 2019 by The Rosen Publishing Group, Inc.

First Edition

Library of Congress Cataloging-in-Publication Data

Names: McGraw, Sean Heather K., author.
Title: How Irish immigrants made America home / Sean Heather K. McGraw.
Description: New York : Rosen Publishing, 2019 | Series: Coming to America: the history of immigration to the United States | Includes bibliographical references and index. | Audience: Grades 5–8.
Identifiers: LCCN 2017050848| ISBN 9781508181262 (library bound) | ISBN 9781508181286 (pbk.)
Subjects: LCSH: Irish—United States—History—Juvenile literature. | Irish Americans—History—Juvenile literature. | Immigrants—United States—History—Juvenile literature.
Classification: LCC E184.I6 M365 2019 | DDC 973/.049162—dc23
LC record available at https://lccn.loc.gov/2017050848

Manufactured in the United States of America

On the cover: Children celebrate their Irish heritage in New York City's 2013 St. Patrick's Day Parade.

CONTENTS

Introduction

IRELAND
just before
THE ENGLISH INVASION

Scale of English Miles
0   10   20   30   40   50   60

Ireland was traditionally divided into five provinces: Ulster, Meath, Leinster, Munster, and Connaught. The Elizabethan reconquest (1588–1610) led to Scottish and English settlers living in Ulster, Meath, and Leinster.

rish and Scots-Irish people, henceforth referred to as the Irish, left all parts of Ireland to immigrate to the United States between the seventeenth and twentieth centuries. A few thousand Irish came in the seventeenth century and settled parts of New England and the mid-Atlantic. These immigrants influenced the political development of the British colonies. They also served as soldiers, statesmen, and farmers. But from the beginning, they were at a disadvantage because negative attitudes influenced how they were treated when they weren't a part of isolated communities.

Then, Scots-Irish from Northern Ireland totaling 250,000 to 500,000 moved to the United States in the eighteenth century because of social, economic, and political hardship.

Almost a million Irish emigrated between 1800 and 1845. The Great Famine of 1845 to 1852, also called the Irish Potato Famine, caused a loss of about half of the population's initial 8 million people. More than 2 million emigrated in that period, and more than 750,000 settled in the United States. The role of the Irish immigrant shifted in this century. The Irish began to serve as the nation's builders, soldiers, domestic servants, and politicians.

Between the 1850s and 1910, almost five million Irish immigrated to the United States. In the first half of the twentieth century, the Irish and Scots-Irish were often victims of cultural and religious prejudice and disastrous English governmental policies.

Understanding the influence of the Irish on the history and culture of the United States is vital to understanding the country's shifting perceptions of race and identity. Race and identity are important to understand because such associations have an impact on one's standing in society, even before a person attempts to achieve any life goals. For example, historically, people of Anglo-Saxon descent in the United States owned businesses that refused to hire people from nondominant race groups—including the Irish. Exclusion from high-paying jobs contributes to poverty.

It is also important for students of history to acknowledge the contributions of people who came from different cultures. Technological, social, and political advancement doesn't happen in a vacuum, and no country has an exclusive ability to innovate. In fact, many inventions and successes occur through international cooperation. However, some readers may not be aware that their country of origin isn't the only place where people have developed technology or worked to advance the rights of the people.

Finally, an outward look at the circumstances that cause people to leave their homelands teaches about the unique perspective of immigrants. Famine, war, and a weak economy are common factors driving emigration, and events like these motivate the actions of immigrants. That is why different immigrant communities, even from the same country, have varying levels of wealth and different demographics.

The Green Fields of Ireland

The Irish settled in prehistoric times on the island in the North Atlantic Ocean. The lush, green fields, numerous rivers and bays, carbon-rich bogs, and rocky cliffs and mountains of Ireland proved a great attraction for many other groups. Those groups' interactions with the Irish were not always peaceful. Various problems and prejudices and cultural shifts have characterized the history of the interactions between the Irish and the Danes, the English, and the Norman-French.

The Irish, or Gaels, are related to other Celtic peoples, like the Ceutrones of ancient Gaul (France). The Ceutrones, known as fierce warriors, are shown here in a meeting with Hannibal, the Carthaginian general.

THE EMERALD ISLE

The island of Ireland is located on the western edge of Europe, just west of the island of Great Britain. Its climate is generally temperate. There is so much rain that the fields are green much of the year, so the island is often called the Emerald Isle.

Over the centuries, Ireland has been the setting of much migration and warfare between various peoples. The earliest were prehistoric Neolithic tribes who lived there ten thousand years ago. Later, Gaelic-speaking Celtic tribes gradually migrated to Ireland over several centuries between 1,000 and 500 BCE from Continental Europe. They assimilated the Neolithic tribes. These people are known as the Gaels. Many of the northern Gaels of Dál Riata, a Gaelic kingdom, also conquered parts of Scotland in the fifth century and ruled and intermixed with the Celtic Picts of Scotland.

Many surnames in English, Scandinavian, and German were originally patronymic. Some include Johnson, Johansen, or Hansen; these all mean "son of John." Irish names were also patronymic. *Mac* also means "son of," so Mac Carthaigh (McCarthy) means "son of Carthaigh." Women were called *iníon mhic,* or "daughter of son," and this was abbreviated to "Nic." "Mac" often became abbreviated to "Mc."

Scottish names also have "Mac" and "Mc," "Nic" and "Ni" because the Scots and Irish are related ethnically. "O" or "Ua" means "grandson," so O Sullivan means "grandson of Suileabhain" ("eye of the god Levan"). The apostrophe in a name like O'Sullivan is a misunderstanding: the English thought it meant "of."

By the twelfth century CE, the Irish population had grown. Both "Mac" and "O" came to more generally describe a descendent of an individual, and the name of the clan became the surname of many people within that clan. In addition, when the Norman-French conquered Ireland in 1169, they gave some of their surnames, such as DeBurgh or Burke, Costello, and Power, to some of the Irish. Today, popular surnames in Ireland are Murphy, Kelly or O'Kelly, and Sullivan or O'Sullivan. Many Irish Americans also carry these names.

Between the eighth and the eleventh centuries, the Norse from Norway and Danes from Denmark conquered large parts of England and founded cities in Ireland, such as Dublin and Galway. And in 1189, the Norman-French, who had already conquered England in 1066, invaded Ireland. Some Anglo-Normans settled there, and many of these settlers eventually intermarried with the native Irish and Viking populace. The settlers came to view themselves as Irish.

After defeating various native Irish lords in Northern Ireland in the early seventeenth century, James I officially began the Plantation of Ulster in Northern Ireland. The plantation's purpose was to provide a loyal population, replace the old lords, and manage the native Irish. Numerous English from the areas of Cumberland and Northumberland and the Scottish from Dumfries, Galloway, and Glasgow migrated to replace the Irish nobility who had been forced to flee. The colonists, called undertakers, were English and Scots who had taken the Oath of Supremacy—the oath of loyalty to King James. They evicted many native Irish from these lands, and some English and Scottish people were given ownership of the land. The new landowners gave tenancy to other English and Scottish people, while the middle class and poor Irish remained as subtenants and servants. Those landowners, the Planters, came to be called Scots-Irish and later, in America, Scotch-Irish. Scottish Presbyterians also came to be called the Ulster Scots.

LAND DESIRE, OWNERSHIP, AND CHANGE

One of the major themes in US history has been colonists' desire to own land. Europeans viewed land and natural resources as a private commodity. Europeans interpreted the Biblical injunction given to Adam to have "dominion" and "subdue" the land and animals as proof that God valued private ownership and use of natural resources. These combined to create an urge for individuals to be able to obtain their own land and natural resources.

The European view of land caused discord even within Europe. In Britain, the lower classes were denied a chance to own farms. It was often the case that obtaining a farm was too expensive or renters charged high rents. This meant that when British and Irish settlers arrived in the colonies, they were eager to obtain land of their own, to farm it independently, and avoid paying rent to anyone else. The desire for land became all consuming for many colonists.

Native Americans, on the other hand, viewed land as a communal resource to be used moderately and shared. Differing views between Europeans and Native Americans concerning land ownership was the basis for many conflicts between the two groups. Colonists often bought land at unfair terms or took it through force from the Native Americans.

In 1620, English Puritans and adventurers, led by Myles Standish (*center*), settled Plymouth Colony, Massachusetts. An early Irish colonist, Daniel Gookin Jr., arrived in 1644 and became a militia officer.

EARLIEST IRISH SETTLERS IN THE COLONIES

The seventeenth century in Great Britain was characterized by war, fire, drought, economic problems, changes in governance, and the persecution of non-Anglicans. The English Civil War of the 1640s and the Williamite War between 1688 and 1691 produced violence, famine, and animosity between the peoples in Ireland. Shortly after that, the Penal Laws were enacted. They forbade Catholics and non-Anglicans such as Presbyterians and Quakers from serving in government or in the army. They also couldn't obtain higher education, vote, have their marriages be recognized by the state, or own land or certain goods. The aim of the laws was to gain an oath of loyalty and a payment of tithes to the Anglican Church. These laws were eventually rescinded, but only for the Presbyterians,

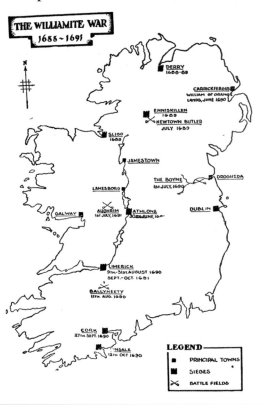

THE WILLIAMITE WAR
1688~1691

DERRY
1688-89

CARRICKFERGUS
WILLIAM OF ORANGE
LANDS, JUNE 1690

ENNISKILLEN
1689
NEWTOWN BUTLER
JULY 1689

SLIGO
1689

JAMESTOWN

THE BOYNE
1st JULY 1690

DROGHEDA

LANESBORO

AUGHRIM
1st JULY, 1691

ATHLONE
30th JUNE 1690

DUBLIN

GALWAY

LIMERICK
9th-31st AUGUST 1690
SEPT.-OCT. 1691

BALLYNEETY
11th AUG. 1690

CORK
27th SEPT. 1690

KINSALE
13th OCT 1690

LEGEND
PRINCIPAL TOWNS
SIEGES
BATTLE FIELDS

The chaotic Williamite War (1688–1691) between King James II and Prince William of Orange caused many Presbyterians to leave Ireland because of the restrictive Penal Laws against them.

Irishman James Logan (1674–1751), secretary to William Penn (founder of Pennsylvania), encouraged Scots-Irish immigration but was disappointed when settlers repeatedly fell into conflict with Native Americans.

by the end of the eighteenth century and for the Catholics by Emancipation in 1829.

The earliest Irish settlers in the American colonies left to escape war, persecution, and economic problems. A few southern Irish, northern Scots-Irish Presbyterians, and Northern Irish Anglicans (Irish-born descendants of English, Anglican settlers) migrated in the seventeenth century to the American continent. One such settler was Daniel Gookin Jr. (1612–1687). His family settled in Massachusetts, and he later became a militia major general and a supervisor of relations with Native Americans. Among others was Charles McCarthy from Cork. He and forty-eight of his countrymen founded East Greenwich, Rhode Island.

A massive migration of Protestant Scots-Irish from Northern Ireland between 1715 and 1745 occurred because of political, social, and economic hardship in Ireland. Once in the American British colonies, this migration produced great geographic expansion for the colonies, largely because of the rivalry between the Scots-Irish settlers, the French, and Native American tribes. Those interactions and rivalries contributed to the American Revolution because the interactions conflicted with the desires of the British crown.

DROUGHT, FAMINE, DISEASE, AND RENT TROUBLES

Aside from political troubles left over from the seventeenth century, the eighteenth century brought on famine and disease. Northern Ireland had had a series of droughts in the 1680s and 1690s that led to crop failures. Crops failed in 1717 and 1718, and a large number of cattle began to suffer from disease. Famines also occurred in 1728, 1729, and 1739.

Beginning in 1718, about 300 Ulster Presbyterians and their ministers fled to Boston. Samuel Shute, the governor of the Massachusetts Bay Colony, granted them land in New Hampshire. From 1725 to 1729, about 3,500 Scots-Irish Protestants from Ulster and Connaught left for the colonies.

In *A History of Ulster*, Jonathan Bardon writes of how a further famine in 1741, produced by bad weather and shortages of seeds, led to "the roads spread with dead and dying bodies." During this time, people faced higher rents and eviction. From the 1740s, about five thousand people emigrated from Ireland every year until 1770. The peak emigration occurred in the 1770s, from 1770 to 1776, when fluctuations in international prices on linen led to an economic crisis. In this era, about forty thousand northern Irish Presbyterians and other Protestants, many of them weavers and their families, emigrated.

FORGING A PATH

Between 1700 and 1820, about 250,000 to 500,000 people from Ireland, the largest nationality of non-English immigrants, arrived in the colonies. There were some Catholics, specifically native "Gaelic Irish," who went to America. This group was primarily made up of male indentured servants. The majority were Protestant Scots-Irish from Northern Ireland.

Scots-Irish New Light Presbyterians founded Princeton College, originally the College of New Jersey, in 1746 in Elizabethtown to train ministers. It was relocated to Princeton, New Jersey, in 1756.

By the 1790 census, the first in the United States, an average of 14 to 17 percent of whites, or at least 440,000 people, were from Ireland or were descendants of Irish immigrants. The majority of them were descended from Presbyterian Scots-Irish people. At least one hundred families went to northern New England (modern-day New Hampshire and Maine) and founded towns named for places in Ulster such as Londonderry, Antrim, and Belfast. Many others settled in the lower Hudson Valley region, where the Dutch had founded New Netherland.

From the Delaware region, the Scots-Irish flooded north to the Susquehanna River valley in Pennsylvania between 1710 and 1731 and spread north and west to the Cumberland Valley between 1725 and 1755. Others moved to the Appalachian Mountains in western Maryland and the Shenandoah Valley of western Virginia between 1727 and 1741. By 1745, many had also moved from Virginia to the Carolinas. In 1736, another segment of new settlers from Northern Ireland moved directly to the Carolinas and Virginia.

Scots-Irish communities early on were Presbyterian. In particular, Presbyterianism incudes the doctrine of predestination, or the idea that a person could not do anything to obtain God's favor because salvation had been decided long before each person's birth. Reverend Francis Makemie (1658–1708) came from Donegal in northwest Ireland in 1683 and set up the first Presbyterian church in the American colonies. As the colonists moved farther west and south, many were unable to attend a Presbyterian church because churches weren't established for that denomination in other places.

Religious divisions arose both among Puritan Congregationalists and Presbyterians. The Great Awakening of the 1730s to 1740s was characterized by a resurgence of religious practice in the colonies, but it was also the cause of sectarian divisions. The Presbyterians founded the College of New Jersey (modern-day Princeton) in New Jersey in 1746, and Hampden-Sydney College in 1776 in Virginia. This enthusiastic advocacy for Christianity became the ancestor of modern preachers and denominations.

APPALACHIAN MOUNTAIN MUSIC

The term "Appalachian music" refers to music from the cultural area of Appalachia. Appalachia is the central and southern portion of the Appalachian mountain range.

In 1916, English composer Cecil Sharpe and American folklorist Olive Dame Campbell decided to travel around the area collecting and transcribing the music of the people. They wanted to capture the music before it was lost to modernization.

Sharpe and Campbell found that this music was a mixture of several influences. Ballad songs,

(continued on the next page)

Suite progressive de Croquis pour l'Étude de la Mine de Plomb.

VALERIO 1852.

The Appalachian mountain dulcimer, a type of zither, is descended from European instruments like the hummel and scheitholz (a hybrid depicted here) and was adopted and transformed by the Scots-Irish.

VISA

UNITED STA

(continued from the previous page)

which told stories of romance, loss, horror, and domesticity, were inherited from the Scots-Irish, Scottish, and English. Some ballad songs include "Barbara Allen" and "Wayfaring Stranger." Similarly, dance reels (fast tunes played on fiddles) were from the Irish, Scottish, and Scots-Irish. Some dance reels include "Cumberland Gap" and "The Siege of Ennis." African influences also contributed rhythms, guitar chords, and instruments. The West African banjo was one such instrument.

While several influences went into Appalachian Mountain music, it also bred new instruments and styles. The mountain dulcimer was invented in Appalachia. It is an instrument with three strings that a player plucks. It may have been derived from European influence.

Radio shows such as the Grand Old Opry (begun in 1925) were a major impetus in blending the old and new styles, with musicians such as Uncle Dave Macon and the Carter Family. Earl Scruggs, of the Bluegrass Boys, and Bill Monroe popularized and innovated the bluegrass style in the 1940s. Kentucky singer and dulcimer player Jean Ritchie preserved many of the older ballads while also writing her own songs protesting strip mining.

FRONTIER SOCIETY, FRONTIERSMEN, AND FARMERS

The Scots-Irish generally tried to maintain their culture, language and speech patterns, kinship patterns, and religion. Still, they often intermarried with the English and Scottish. The Scots-Irish frontiersmen who settled the wilderness from Pennsylvania to Georgia became famous for their individualism, ferocity in battles with the Native Americans, and ability to survive in a harsh environment. Likewise, speech patterns in Appalachia retain some sense of their origin as Scots-Irish, such as "we all, you all, what all," and "I used to could" (I was able to). And in Pennsylvania, words like "fireboard" for "mantelpeice," "you'ns" for "you all," and "hull" for "to shell" caught on among the communities there.

Women did most of the household chores, just as they did in Ireland. Among other chores, they cooked, washed, sewed, milked cows, churned butter, ground corn, and administered medicine. They also did gardening, dyed and carded wool and flax, spun and weaved cloth, and preserved food. They raised the children and often were the main source of religious instruction, especially in areas where there was a shortage of churches and ministers.

Although their work was essential to maintaining the health of the family, women had very few legal rights. They could not vote or own property. They could not attend school

DAVY CROCKETT

David "Davy" Crockett (1786–1836) is known as the King of the Wild Frontier. His life exemplifies the nomadic and challenging existence of the frontiersmen. His family struggled to sustain itself. They moved several times and tried to earn the means to survive by farming and operating a mill and a tavern.

In 1813, Crockett enlisted as a scout for Francis Jones's Company of Mounted Riflemen during the War of 1812. Crockett fought in the Creek War (1813–1814) against the Red Stick Creek band who had allied themselves with the British and Spanish during the War of 1812. This group was unhappy with the trade imbalance that favored Americans.

In 1824, Crockett became a congressional representative and focused on the needs of poor men. Out of respect for the Native Americans, he voted against Andrew Jackson's Indian Removal Act. The decision to vote against the Indian Removal Act was so unpopular that it caused him to not be reelected. Crockett disliked Jackson and his successor, Martin Van Buren, so he decided to raise a volunteer force to go to Texas. He became involved in the insurrection against Mexico. This rebellion culminated in his death at the Battle of the Alamo in February 1836.

or take a job of their choice. But they could sometimes exercise authority over marriage dowry money to fulfill their interests. Generally, husbands had social control over them. Children were subordinate to their parents and helped them with their work. Most children in these communities did not go to school because there were few schools and teachers.

THE SCOTS-IRISH, SLAVES, AND NATIVE AMERICANS

Before 1815, in many places, the Scots-Irish had arrived as lower-class indentured servants. After their manumission, they were still unable to purchase slaves. As David Noel Doyle writes in *Making the Irish American: History and Heritage of the Irish in the United States*, the majority of Scots-Irish were not slave owners before 1815. However, a few were slave owners from the earliest colonial times. Doyle explains how in the 1750s, the Scots-Irish community in Cub Creek, Virginia, had a few people who owned five slaves or more. After about 1815, there began to be more Scots-Irish slave owners who owned small plantations with a few slaves. Large landowners who owned hundreds of slaves, such as Andrew Jackson, also increased. Slavery was the vehicle through which Scots-Irish wealth increased.

Scots-Irish settlers inevitably encountered Native Americans. Sometimes their contact was friendly. However, earlier distrust and hostilities resurfaced. Naturally, the reason involved the land. Many settlers bought their land from the same government that negotiated rights to certain lands from the Native Americans. But many could not afford to purchase it or did not want to purchase it and so instead simply squatted on the land.

In 1754, the French and Indian War broke out. The British, the French, and each side's allies competed for control over the Ohio River valley. Native American tribes fought as allies on both sides with the hopes of winning favorable land and trading terms from either the French or the English. The

Major General Edward Braddock and his troops, including George Washington, were defeated during the French and Indian War near Fort Duquesne in the Ohio Valley in 1755.

Natives also attacked the settlers in revenge for their having usurped their land and hunting rights. The frontier settlers retaliated. The Scots-Irish also fought, but only alongside the British. At the end of the conflict, the Treaty of Paris of 1763 set a boundary between the settlers and the Native Americans. The settlers did not like this and continued to encroach on Native American lands.

The French and Indian War caused massive debt for Britain. To offset this debt, the British government gradually began creating tax and regulation increases for the colonists. The British government reasoned that charging the colonists was fair because the war was a conflict that was meant to benefit the colonists. However, these changes sparked resentment among all the colonists and eventually led to the decision to declare independence in 1776.

The Scots-Irish were prominent in the events leading up to and battles during the war. Thousands of soldiers and officers were Scots-Irish. For example, the signers of the Declaration of Independence who were Irish born or had Irish ancestry included Matthew Thornton, George Taylor, James Smith, Edward Rutledge, Thomas Lynch, Thomas McKean, George Read, and Charles Carroll.

The Great Hunger

Previous generations of immigrants were primarily Protestant, but when the Great Famine occurred in 1845, the characteristics of the immigrants changed. These new Irish immigrants were Catholic and often Gaelic speaking. The religious and cultural distrust between the Catholic and Protestant Irish led to animosity in the United States. What followed were violent episodes of cultural intolerance.

THE BAD TIMES

Between 1845 and 1852, most Irish people in Ireland did not own the land they lived on. Instead, about ten thousand Anglo-Irish and British landowners, many of whom were absentee owners, owned the land. These landowners leased the land to farmers, who controlled more than 30 acres (12 hectares). These influential farmers subsequently further subdivided the property and leased and rented those smaller parcels of land.

There had also been a population boom between 1780 and 1820. The population increased from 4 million in 1788 to 8.2 million in 1841. As a result, more and more people received smaller parcels of land to farm.

In addition, during this period, many landlords evicted people off the land. They also replaced common farming land with land for grazing animals. Northern Ireland was the only area that had any substantial industry at all.

Finally, in the late eighteenth century, the potato became the most cultivated crop throughout Ireland, especially in the south and west. Potatoes were an especially convenient crop because they could feed a whole family.

The increased population, lack of a diversified economy, loss of access to cultivable land, and the overreliance on a single crop produced a catastrophe. The Great Hunger came in 1845.

The problem began when a fungus, *Phytophthora infestans*, appeared on potatoes in the fall of 1845. The fungus caused potatoes to shrivel up on the outside and rot on the inside. It was a massive crop failure that was agitated by the economic choices of landowners.

This family looks on its blighted potato crop in despair. The Great Hunger of 1845 to 1852 caused massive starvation, death, and emigration, particularly to the United States.

People had no cash or potatoes or ability to work to pay their rents, so this was the cause of the clearances, or the landlords evicting many people. From there, starvation, weather, and disease were all that was left for the impoverished masses. Though the government provided some aid through soup kitchens and paid work on construction projects between 1845 and 1847, it wasn't enough. The several private famine-relief funds were also not enough to handle the people's needs. Around 1.1 to 1.5 million people starved to death and died of diseases. The famine lasted until 1852.

A FIRSTHAND ACCOUNT OF THE FAMINE

Asenath Nicholson was an American Quaker and a widow from Vermont who had been a schoolteacher. She visited Ireland and decided to set up a soup kitchen to help feed some of the poor. This excerpt comes from her book *Annals of the Famine in Ireland in 1847, 1848, 1849*, published in 1851. In this description, she illustrates the misery caused by starvation and eviction: "[A landlord] showed no mercy to a poor man that was toilin' for the potato; but as soon as the famine was sore on the craturs, he drove every one into the blake staurm that could not give the rent, and many's the poor bein' that died with the starvation."

THE PASSAGE OVER

Around 2.1 million people emigrated from Ireland because of the famine. More than 780,000 went to the United States directly. Those who could afford the move to North America often left from Irish ports such as Cork. But many were only able to secure passage from Liverpool, in England, and had to incur additional costs to get there.

Because it was cheaper to buy a ticket to Canada, many thousands landed there, in Quebec and Montreal. Most of those who survived traveled south to the United States.

Around thirty thousand of those who left for Canada in 1847 alone died either while on the ship or soon after arrival. The rate of death on these ships was so high that they

VISA

Castle Garden (West Battery Fort), New York City, the nation's first immigrant holding center, was established to stop predatory situations against Irish immigrants. It processed eight million people between 1855 and 1890.

became known as coffin ships. Robert Smith testified before the government that these ships were overcrowded, filthy, and riddled with disease and that the passengers lacked food, water, and even the ability to stand up very often.

Most of the passengers landed at New York City; Philadelphia, Pennsylvania; and Boston, Massachusetts. Some went to southern cities. New York City began regulating immigrants in 1855 with the establishment of Castle Garden. This institution attempted to provide immigrants with honest information and advice. Other cities had their own approach to regulating immigration and processing immigrants because the federal government did not regulate immigration until the Ellis Island immigrant checkpoint was created in 1892.

PREJUDICE AGAINST THE IRISH

Prejudice increased as Irish immigration increased in the 1830s and 1840s. Protestants, already wary of Catholics, came to distrust Catholic Irish people even more than they had disliked the Presbyterian Irish. Between the 1830s and 1860s, Presbyterian Irish gradually lost much of the prejudice attached to them as the English focused on the differences between Protestantism and Catholicism. It came to be that Presbyterian Irish people felt that they were more Protestant than Irish.

The problem became one of violently low tolerance. In 1844, Catholics requested that the Philadelphia public school system use the Douay–Rheims Bible rather than the Protestant King James version of the Bible for schoolchildren. This request led to riots in the Kensington and Southwark districts of Philadelphia. Nativists who opposed the Catholic Irish demographic burned sixty homes and two churches. More than 24 nativists died in the riot, and 150 Catholics were injured.

The growing nativism against Catholic Irish influenced the development of political parties in the United States. The Know-Nothing Party, so called because their members were instructed to say they "knew nothing" about the party's doings to outsiders, fielded very popular candidates in the 1856 state

VISA
UNITED STA

Millard Fillmore, who served as president from 1850 to 1853, disliked immigrants and Catholics. He ran for president, unsuccessfully, on the 1856 nativist Know-Nothing Party ticket.

elections. Members of this party, including most Protestant Scots-Irish, eventually formed one of the major bases of the Republican Party that emerged around the time of the 1860 presidential election. The English and Protestant Irish also became Republicans. The Catholic Irish, who had joined Jackson's Democratic Party in the 1820s and 1830s, remained with that party.

LOSSES

The famine produced great losses for Irish culture. By 1845, about half of the population consisted of monolingual Gaelic speakers. But the deaths of a million, many of whom were Gaelic speakers, and the immigration of millions more produced a greater loss of the language, especially in the United States. The Irish were encouraged to speak English to get along with other Americans, so they often spoke English exclusively to assimilate. The overall community in the United States retained a few expressions, proverbs, and words while complete fluency in Gaelic was lost.

In the famine era, a tradition called the American wake evolved. Like a traditional Irish wake, attendees would mourn immigrants. In an American wake, they mourned the immigrants before they left the country in the same fashion in which they mourned the dead. They extended this tradition to celebrate immigrants because it was unlikely that relatives and friends would ever see them again, especially elderly immigrants. People gathered to talk, sing, drink, eat, and tell stories before the final goodbye.

Irish foods have changed, too. While the potato is no longer the staple of the Irish diet, it is still firmly associated with the Irish. The traditional cabbage and beef stew that is eaten in America on St. Patrick's Day was originally cabbage and bacon. However, beef was cheaper in the United States. The custom of eating barmbrack, a bread with raisins or sultanas, is a Halloween tradition. Baked in the barmbrack were typically a pea, a stick, a piece of cloth, a coin, and a ring. Respectively, whoever received each of these items in his or her piece would know their fortune for the coming year; would abstain from marriage; have an unhappy marriage; have bad luck or good fortune; or get married.

Halloween used to be a pre-Christian seasonal festival called Samhain, or All Souls' Night, and it marked the start of winter. Samhain honored the dead and regarded them with fear. Participants believed that the dead, goblins, witches, and evil demons rose to bother the living. An extra plate was set out for the ghosts of dead relatives and friends at the table. Dressing as a demon, ghost, or witch could ward off evil beings, as could reciting various prayers and carving frightening images in turnips. In the United States, because of the availability of pumpkins, the Irish used them instead of turnips. Despite Halloween having been commercialized and adopted by Americans of all ethnic heritages, it remains one of the most recognizably Celtic contributions to US culture.

CHAPTER FOUR

Irish Work and Domestic Life, 1850s to 1910

B etween the 1850s and 1910, the Irish became the major immigrant group in cities throughout the East Coast. They labored in construction and in factories and as domestic servants. Religious sisters became teachers, social workers, and nurses. Some even headed out to the Midwest and the West. This feat made them one of the largest immigrant groups in western cities.

LIFE IN IRISH NEIGHBORHOODS

The living spaces that immigrants found were often windowless cellars and dirty tenements without running water. These were places infested with vermin, and several families were often crowded into a single apartment. Irish neighborhoods like the Five Points area of the Sixth Ward in New York City quickly earned a reputation as places of disease, violence, and degradation.

Most immigrants stayed in the cities where they landed. By the 1870s, almost half of Irish immigrants lived in cities with a population of twenty-five thousand or more. These immigrants usually found homes with others from their county— if possible, with their own relatives. And, because Irish

This street, Donovan Lane, also called Murderer's Alley, is an example of the crime, poverty, squalor, and homelessness rampant in the mostly Irish neighborhood of Five Points in New York City.

men could vote for the first time, they quickly rose up the ranks of the Democratic Party to become influential in politics.

THE FIGHTING IRISH: THE CIVIL WAR

The Irish and Scots-Irish, including both Irish born and those with Irish ancestry, fought on both sides of the Civil War. There were Confederate Irish units from Virginia, South Carolina, North Carolina, Texas, Georgia, and other states. Many were recruited directly off the boat when recruiters offered them money for their service. The Irish made up the largest number of foreign-born troops. Because of the great Irish presence in the war, Irish immigrants often found themselves fighting other Irish immigrants.

The Union's Fighting Sixty-Ninth regiment, raised by Colonel Michael Corcoran, lost many at the battle of Bull Run. The regiment was incorporated in the Irish Brigade, led by Thomas Francis Meagher. They fought at Gettysburg, the Second Battle of Bull Run, Antietam, Fredericksburg, and Chancellorsville.

Even an Irish woman fought in the Civil War in the First Michigan Cavalry: Bridget Divers, whose husband was wounded. She not only served as a nurse but also galloped into action with a rifle and rallied the regiment to halt the Union retreat at the Battle of Fair Oaks.

Despite their involvement, many Irish people did not want to fight.

By 1863, the war had become more dangerous and entrenched. There was a new army draft. One provision of this draft was that wealthy people could avoid serving by purchasing the substitution of a poor man. Usually, the Irish were the poor people who were forced into the draft when the rich paid their way out of serving. Also, the Irish objected to the Emancipation Proclamation. They were afraid that black people might take their jobs. This time, the Irish weren't going to go along with the new draft.

Irish rioters fought Union army troops in New York City after the Conscription Act of 1863 was announced in July. Hundreds were killed and injured, and property and buildings were destroyed.

The Irish started the New York City Draft Riots of 1863 in July of that year. Irish workers attacked recruitment centers, government buildings, and the offices of the Republican Party. They also beat and lynched many black people and burned down the Colored Orphan Asylum.

The riot lasted for four days. A regiment of the Union army, including many Irish soldiers, was called out to stop the rioting.

MALE LABOR

Just like the Irish of the earlier nineteenth century, most Irish immigrants from the 1850s to 1910 lacked the knowledge to do skilled labor. Most men found work as manual laborers. They built many of the buildings in eastern cities that went up at that time, just as they had helped dig canals in earlier decades, including New York's Erie Canal and the Farmington Canal in Connecticut. The continued expansion and rebuilding of cities was done with a lot of Irish labor.

The Irish were one ethnic group who mined the anthracite coal mines of Pennsylvania. Many Irish workers also built the railroads from the East to Promontory Point, Utah, while the Chinese built the railroad from San Francisco to Promontory Point. Those railroads were joined in 1869.

As the Irish moved to the Midwest and West, they gradually obtained more skilled and white-collar jobs. Also, experience in the Civil War often led to Irish soldiers becoming police officers and firefighters.

Irish women were leaders of the women's assemblies in the Knights of Labor workers' organization. These delegates to the 1886 Knights of Labor convention helped create better conditions for workers.

Irish men were prominent in the American labor movement. Two out of every three railroad strikers of 1877 were Irish. Irishmen began the Workingmen's Benevolent Association, a union for the coal miners of Pennsylvania, and P. J. McGuire, the father of Labor Day, was a first-generation American of Irish descent who helped to start the American Federation of Labor (AFL) in 1886. Labor activists fought for the rights of workers through boycotting, voting, strikes, and even violence.

Twenty-two US presidents have descended at least partially from Scots-Irish or Irish heritage. Some of them include Andrew Jackson, Theodore Roosevelt, Woodrow Wilson, Grover Cleveland, and Barack Obama. All of those who came from Scots-Irish or Irish heritage were Protestant, except John F. Kennedy, who was Catholic. Andrew Jackson (served from 1829 to 1837) and James K. Polk (1845–1849) increased the boundaries of the United States.

Jackson, a Democrat, was a military general who led forces to defeat the Creek and Seminole tribes. He also enabled the United States to annex Florida, a formerly Spanish territory. As president, he signed the Indian Removal Act of 1830, allowing for the forced removal of the Cherokee and other tribes from southern states to Oklahoma. The Trail of Tears, as the removal and subsequent journey to Oklahoma was called, lasted from 1831 until 1850. About four thousand people died on the difficult overland route. American settlers took over the lands that the Cherokee were forced to leave behind.

In 1672, Robert Pollock and his wife, from Northern Ireland, settled in Maryland; they were the ancestors of President James K. Polk. Polk believed in Manifest Destiny, the belief that Americans were virtuous and that God intended the United States

(continued on the next page)

President Grover Cleveland was of Anglo-Irish descent. He was known as a strong opponent of corrupt Tammany Hall politics.

(continued from the previous page)

to control all the land from the Atlantic to the Pacific coast. He helped start the Mexican-American War, which lasted from 1846 to 1848. It resulted in the annexation of California and the territory that became the southwestern states.

FEMALE LABOR

From the nineteenth century to the 1930s, most Irish women worked in domestic services, the needle trades, and as factory workers. These women started working as teenagers, some as young as twelve years old.

Many working women were homesick and spent their free time practicing Catholicism, especially attending Mass. Masses and other church events were some of the few times these women could be with other Irish people. There, they could meet friends they could relate to and find prospective husbands.

Irish domestic servants were at first stereotyped as ignorant, awkward, lazy, defiant, and bad tempered. However, because few native-born Americans would undertake domestic service and factory work, Irish women invariably became the main servant class until after World War I. Melissa Josefiak writes in "'The Woman Came To Do Laundry…': Depression-

Era Domestic Servants in Greater Hartford, Connecticut" about how the number of black women working as domestic workers overtook the Irish. They worked from about five in the morning to nine at night, and some were on call all the time. Their tasks involved caring for young children, cleaning, and cooking. Time off was limited to one afternoon a week. They received room and board and enough earnings to save money to bring relatives over, to educate relatives, to marry, and to raise children.

By the late nineteenth century, Irish women had also achieved prominence as stenographers, secretaries, and teachers. By 1910, there were two thousand second-generation female Irish teachers out of the seven thousand female teachers in New York City. These Irish schoolteachers were upwardly mobile. They succeeded in bringing their children up in greater wealth and education than ever before.

Irishwomen were also heavily involved in the labor and union movements. Mary Kenny O'Sullivan helped organize the AFL in the 1890s, and Mary Harris Jones (1837–1930), also known as Mother Jones, worked in the labor movement for decades and helped found the Industrial Workers of the World (IWW).

PILLARS OF SOCIETY

Sisters, or religious women who had taken vows different from a nun's, were pioneers of educational and social welfare in the United States. In the late nineteenth century, they also fought for higher education for Catholic women.

The Sisters of Mercy, the Sisters of the Presentation of the Blessed Mary, the Sisters of the Congregation of St. Joseph of Peace, and other orders staffed schools, hospitals, orphanages, and charitable organizations. They also served as role models for Irishwomen and supplemental administrators for the Catholic hierarchy. They visited prisons, formed medical relief groups during disease outbreaks, and were the vanguard of Catholic efforts to prevent Protestant orphan societies from taking Irish orphans and converting them.

The Sisters of Mercy arrived in New York in the 1840s. Between then and 1900, many thousands of nuns arrived from Ireland to devote their lives to helping the poor. Margaret Anna Cusack, the founder of the Sisters of the Congregation of St. Joseph of Peace, founded her order specifically to train Irish girls for domestic service and to help them navigate the difficulties of being an immigrant.

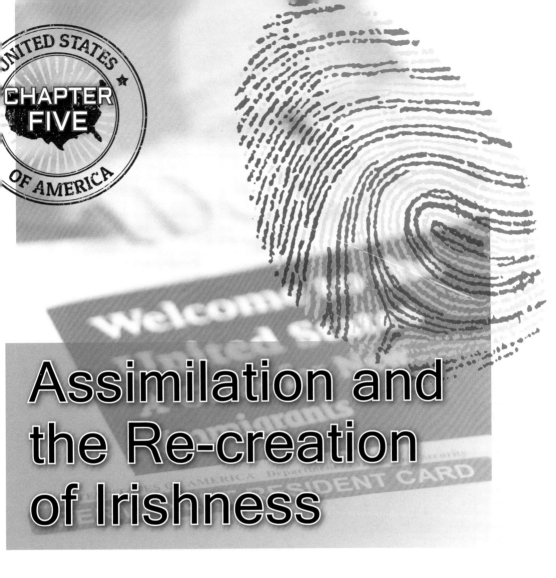

Assimilation and the Re-creation of Irishness

The twentieth century was the period when the Irish obtained full acceptance and were assimilated into American culture. At the same time, they created great political, social, and cultural changes. The contributions of the Irish took the form of involvement in the government and in the arts.

Politician William M. "Boss" Tweed (1823–1878), leader of Democratic politics in Tammany Hall in New York City, was notorious for fraud, but he also spent great sums helping Irish immigrants.

VISA
UNITED STA

HOW THE IRISH BECAME WHITE

There had always been a racial hierarchy of peoples that placed Anglo-Saxons/English people (and sometimes the Germans of Pennsylvania) above to the Irish, African Americans, Native Americans, and Asians. The Irish were often viewed as both white and nonwhite, and as non-European and European. But the Irish were proactive in making themselves appeal to the white identity.

While the non-Irish English/Anglo-Saxons in the United States viewed the Irish on the same level as black people, the Irish themselves transformed their thinking once they immigrated to the United States. The Irish felt that their hard work, menial jobs, and their historical position as poor, politically colonized people was a kind of slavery. They believed that the English were the ones who had enslaved them. Once in the United States, bosses and Protestants in general continued that sort of slavery. Despite relating to the oppressed position of black slaves in the United States, the Irish developed the attitude that they were better than black people—the Irish were just glad they weren't at the bottom of the social hierarchy.

The Irish came to see themselves as white for another reason. The Irish were afraid that if black people were freed from slavery they would take away jobs from the Irish. This was in line with how many English Protestants felt. The

English then began to accept the Irish as white because they wanted an ally. It was for this reason that the Irish voted for the proslavery Democratic Party en masse throughout the early nineteenth century.

After emancipation, while the Democratic Party could no longer be proslavery, the party still harbored an interest in keeping black people in the bottom rung of society. The Irish, in their own uncomfortable social and economic position, found themselves in intense competition with black people for jobs and social clout. Further, the service of the Irish in the war allowed many to become citizens and vote. Gradually, through the 1860s and 1870s, heavy labor by the Irish was compared favorably to the war record of the Irish.

By the 1870s to 1880s, another cause ensured that the Irish, though still discriminated against and regarded as inferior, were brought in more wholeheartedly to be regarded as white. During those decades, an influx of new immigrants from southern and eastern Europe overshadowed the previous doubts about Irish immigrants' whiteness. This meant that even though the Irish still weren't regarded by white society as well as the English, they were seen as better than the poor, uneducated, and religiously different southern and eastern Europeans. Therefore, the hierarchy stretched to make the Irish into white people by 1900 through their own self-identification and the identification of English Americans. And as white people, they were now easily able and eager to participate in the historical harms white Americans have done to people of color.

THE TWENTIETH CENTURY

World War I, US immigration laws from the 1920s, the Great Depression, and World War II slowed or intentionally restricted immigration. However, the Irish began to thrive in the United States in the first half of the twentieth century. They became more educated and wealthy. Creating more unions meant there was more protection and higher wages for workers. The Irish achieved more parity with Protestants and those of Anglo-Saxon origin.

The Irish had been able to consolidate their control over the governments of many American cities. As a result, they were also able to work their way farther into the political and social fabric of the nation. The Irish were prominent participants in the Democratic Party. Politicians such as Mayor Richard Daley of Chicago; Al Smith, who ran for president in 1928; and John F. Kennedy, who became the thirty-fifth president of the United States in 1961, were known for both their Irish heritage and their political accomplishments.

THE KENNEDY FAMILY

Joseph P. Kennedy, the father of John F. Kennedy, was the descendent of a Great Famine refugee. Through their political and business dealings, including contributing to the speculation crisis that

(continued on the next page)

(continued from the previous page)

caused the stock market crash of 1929 and gaining exclusive rights to import whisky, the Kennedys had amassed a huge fortune. This fortune allowed Joseph P. Kennedy to finance John F. Kennedy's political campaigns.

In the 1960 presidential campaign, Kennedy made the question of his religion a nonissue by stating up front that he believed in a separation of church and state and would not let his Catholicism

John F. Kennedy, the only Irish Catholic to become president, delivers a speech during his presidential campaign on September 27, 1960.

interfere in his presidency. He won by a narrow margin. His victory was the first and only time a Catholic became president. John F. Kennedy's success paved the way for his brother Robert to become attorney general and another brother, Edward, to become a senator. Other family members went into politics as well.

Many Irish had served in the military in World War II and therefore could take advantage of the Servicemen's Readjustment Act of 1944, also known as the GI Bill. By the 1950s, they also participated in the rapid suburbanization of the United States. An exodus of Irish from their traditional strongholds in the urban Northeast and Midwest occurred at the same time as more and more Americans settled in the West and the South. As a result, many neighborhoods stopped being noticeably Irish.

Social mobility and education, largely at Catholic colleges, produced more highly educated people going into law, teaching, and business, as well as police and firefighting jobs. Irish immigration in the United States fell into decline from the 1950s to the 1970s. By 1960, most Irish Americans were third- and fourth-generation Americans. The downside to the Irish becoming Americanized was that it accelerated the loss of Irish culture. Now, Irish people were more American than ever before.

IRISHNESS REEMERGES

The twentieth century saw composers from the vaudeville days of the late nineteenth and early twentieth centuries add to the older Irish folk and ballad traditions. Composers like Chauncey Olcott wrote new Irish songs, which then came to be considered traditional. Notable titles include "My Wild Irish Rose," from 1909, and "When Irish Eyes Are Smiling," from 1912.

Popular singers such as the tenor John McCormack, Ada Jones, Nora Bayes, and Bing Crosby made the crossover into recorded music and popularized Irish American and traditional songs for a wider audience. Beginning in the 1960s, a folk music revival in Ireland, England, and the United States created a huge transatlantic market. Irish musicians including Tommy Makem and the Clancy Brothers brought traditional Irish music back to the United States. This sparked innovations among Irish musicians, who merged traditional and rock music, such as those of Irish Americans groups Black 47, Dropkick Murphys, and Cherish the Ladies.

Since American society decided to begin viewing Irish people as assimilated American white people, preserving the Irish identity required reclaiming their difference. Many Irish have become interested in genealogy and their own family trees. Genealogical and cultural programs, societies, academic programs, and tours have been established to reconnect Irish Americans with their heritage. One pioneer in this endeavor was Mícheál Ó Lócháin. In an ad he purchased in the Irish American newspaper the *Irish World* in 1872, he made the case for Irish people to start reclaiming their language. He began

EXCERPT FROM FRANK McCOURT'S *ANGELA'S ASHES*

Frank McCourt wrote about his childhood in Limerick. He grew up in the 1930s with his alcoholic father, depressed mother, siblings, and abusive schoolteacher. McCourt wrote contemptuously of his father. He also wrote contemptuously of his schoolmaster, a person who valued loyalty and martyrdom to Catholicism above the welfare of children. McCourt wrote of his predicament:

> *The master says it's a glorious thing to die for the Faith and Dad says it's a glorious thing to die for Ireland and I wonder if there's anyone in the world who would like us to live. My brothers are dead and my sister is dead and I wonder if they died for Ireland or the Faith. Dad says they were too young to die for anything. Mam says it was disease and starvation and him never having a job. Dad says, Och, Angela, puts on his cap and goes for a long walk.*

to teach Gaelic classes in Boston in 1873 and founded the Philo-Celtic Society.

The effort caught on. In the 1980s and 1990s, several university Irish and Celtic studies programs were established to train people in the language and culture, at Boston College, New York University, and elsewhere. Similarly, Michael Flatley's *Riverdance* and *Lord of the Dance* in the 1990s significantly changed traditional Irish step dancing. The programs merged traditional dancing with tap, line dancing, use of the arms, and a huge reliance on synchronization and percussion. These changes created a uniquely Irish American form of dancing.

The solidarity and division that immigrants face forms a massive part of the history of the United States. What those relationships leave is a complicated story of trying to get along in a new place and striving to be successful in a competitive environment. Being Irish in the United States has had two distinct flavors for several decades now. But while the Irish community has been accepted by white culture at large, such recognition doesn't eliminate the reoccurring difficulties of life. For example, if a new nationwide economic hardship emerges, unemployment will rise, and an unhealthy domestic political environment can endanger the welfare of a country's citizens of all ethnicities. But when people in a society choose to work together to achieve common goals, they create much more than people working against each other.

MYTH

The Irish are primarily a red-haired, green-eyed, freckled people.

FACT

While red hair is more common among the Irish than among other European peoples, only a small minority of Irish people have red hair. Lots of Irish people have dark hair, and blond hair and blue eyes are extremely prevalent too.

MYTH

The Irish are all alcoholics. They were born with this problem.

FACT

Alcoholism has indeed become a problem for the Irish. Prejudicial treatment of the Irish at the hands of the English and Americans has caused some to turn to the self-destructive habit of drinking too much. Ireland's historically difficult economic problems have also contributed. However, there is nothing innate in the Irish ethnicity that causes alcoholism.

Not all Irish people are alcoholics. Rates of alcoholism are limited only to one's ability to acquire alcohol. Another factor contributing to alcoholism is stress. But people who can afford alcohol and people who encounter stress don't always become alcoholics. In other words, alcoholism isn't easy to predict. It certainly doesn't apply to any ethnicity in particular.

(continued on the next page)

(continued from the previous page)

MYTH

The Irish are all corrupt politically. They are unworthy of trust.

FACT

The notion that Irish people are corrupt comes from the reputation of New York's Tammany Hall. Tammany Hall once provided social, economic, and political support to Irish immigrants, especially those who had no support. It became infamous for corruption because it organized the embezzlement of millions of taxpayer dollars and committed bribery.

Distrust of the Irish also comes from nativist attempts to defame the Irish. Fear that more Irish immigrants seeking jobs would lead to American unemployment motivated the desire to defame the Irish. Nationalism also caused the Irish to be a less desired group because there was a period in American history in which they weren't considered white.

IRISH AMERICANS

Irish Americans and Politics
Twenty-two American presidents were Irish or Scots-Irish American. Twenty-one were Protestant, and one was Catholic.

The Irish were prominent participants in the Democratic Party, including such notable politicians as Mayor Richard Daley of Chicago; Al Smith, a governor of New York who ran for president in 1928; and the Kennedy family, including Joseph P. Kennedy and his son President John F. Kennedy.

Irish Americans and the Civil War
The Civil War saw Irish Americans fighting in both the Confederate and Union armies. Some famous officers were General Patrick Cleburne (Confederate), Colonel Michael Corcoran (who raised the Fighting Sixty-Ninth Regiment, Union), and Thomas Francis Meagher (who led the Irish Brigade, Union).

Holidays
Halloween, or All Souls' Night, was based on a pre-Christian commemoration of the dead and of the supernatural, called Samhain, celebrated in Ireland.

Irish Americans in the Workforce
Irish men between 1820 and 1890 built the Erie Canal as well as canals in Hartford, Farmington, and Enfield, Connecticut.

They also worked in Pennsylvania coal mines and built the railroads from the East Coast to Promontory Point, Utah.

The majority of domestic servants, nannies, maids, and cooks between the 1820s and the 1920s were Irish.

Irish Americans and Organized Labor

Early Irish American union organizers and labor leaders include Mary Harris "Mother" Jones, Mary Kenny O'Sullivan, Leonora O'Reilly, John Siney, John Welsh, Robert Blissert, and P. J. McGuire.

Irish Americans and the Arts

Prominent Irish American writers include Eugene O'Neill (*The Iceman Cometh*, *Long Day's Journey into Night*), Frank McCourt (*Angela's Ashes, Tis'*), Mary Higgins Clark (*Aspire to the Heavens*, *Where Are the Children?*), and Thomas Cahill (*How the Irish Saved Civilization*).

Irish American musicians and songwriters have figured prominently in the American song tradition. Some of the most notable include Chauncey Olcott ("My Wild Irish Rose," "When Irish Eyes are Smiling") and George Cohan ("Over There," "Yankee Doodle Dandy," and "You're a Grand Old Flag").

10,000 BCE The earliest Neolithic peoples are living in Ireland.

500 BCE Celtic tribes take over Ireland.

1609 CE The official Plantation of Ulster with Scottish and English families under King James I is established.

1640s The earliest Irish settlers reach the American British colonies. They founded settlements in Maryland, Delaware, and East Greenwich, Rhode Island.

1683 Reverend Francis Makemie settles in Rehobeth, Maryland, and founds the first Presbyterian church in the Americas.

1717 A massive wave of Ulster Scots-Irish immigration to America begins.

1730s The Great Awakening begins. Religious fervor splits the Presbyterian and Congregational (Puritan) Churches and allows for an increase in Methodists and Baptists.

1754 The French and Indian War begins.

1776 The American Revolutionary War begins.

1844 The Philadelphia Nativist Riots occur. Dozens are killed, hundreds injured, and many homes and churches burned down.

1845 The Great Famine begins. This starts the massive wave of Irish Catholics who will immigrate to the United States during the next sixty years.

1855 Castle Garden, a New York City government agency, is established to regulate immigration to New York City.

1863 The New York City Draft Riots occur. Irishmen who are angry about being drafted into the Civil War and the emancipation of black slaves engage in violence in the streets. They lynch and beat many African Americans.

1869 The first transcontinental railroad is completed in Promontory Point, Utah. Irish Americans contributed significantly to the construction of the eastern portion of the railroad.

1936 Irish American writer Eugene O'Neill is awarded the Nobel Prize for Literature.

1944 The Servicemen's Readjustment Act, also known as the GI Bill, is passed, helping war veterans, including many Irish Americans, to attend college.

1960 Irish Catholic John F. Kennedy is elected as the thirty-fifth president of the United States.

2011 The New York City St. Patrick's Day Parade celebrates its 250th anniversary.

absentee owner A person who owns something, usually land, without living on it or using it.

coffin ships The ships on which Irish emigrants sailed that were infested with vermin and disease, were very cramped, had no fresh air, and ensured that thousands would die either on the ship or shortly after arriving.

defame To cause someone to lose their good reputation.

denomination A branch of a religion in which its followers all adhere to specified beliefs and practices.

doctrine A belief that is central to a religion.

embezzlement Stealing money from a group's funds.

emigrant A person who leaves his or her home country.

eviction Being forced to move out of a home or other rented space because the tenant cannot afford to pay.

Gaelic The language spoken by the Celts in Ireland, the Isle of Man, and the Scottish Highlands.

heritage Something that someone inherits from someone else, either property or culture.

immigrate To permanently come to live in a country that is not one's native country.

indentured servant A servant who offered his or her labor for a set number of years, often in order to secure passage to the colonies or to secure a job.

manumission Receiving freedom from slavery.

nativism The belief that people born in a country should receive services from the country's government and jobs that businesses have to offer before immigrants. Nativism may also appear in the sentiment of not wanting immigrants to enter the country.

natural resources Materials that come from nature.

patronymic A name derived from a male ancestor (often a father).

Presbyterian Relating to a Reformed Protestant church in which member churches adhere to a particular administrative structure. The faith tradition originated in the British Isles, particularly Scotland.

sectarian Limited to certain denominations of a religion.

solidarity Togetherness; acting as a collective group to meet common goals, or expressing agreement for someone's goals.

suburbanization The increase in the population who have moved from cities and rural neighborhoods to neighborhoods on the peripheries of cities, known as suburbs.

American Irish Historical Society
991 5th Avenue
New York, NY 10028
(212) 288-2263
Website: http://aihs.org
Facebook: @AmericanIrishHS
This organization, founded in 1897, has a library and
    archives, as well as an exhibition and fundraising events.
    It seeks to spread awareness of Irish history and provide a
    venue for people to understand more about Irish history
    and culture.

Children of Ireland Group
PO Box 13241
Tallahassee, FL 32317
(850) 562-6466 Ext. 3307
Website: http://www.childrenofireland.us
The Children of Ireland Group raises funds to assist children
    and teens in Northern Ireland by helping to establish
    children's centers, after-school programs, mentorship
    programs, and antigang and antidrug programs.

Daltaí na Gaeilge
279 Park Avenue
Elberon, NJ 07740-4530
(732) 571-1988
Website: http://daltai.com
Daltaí na Gaeilge was founded to provide Irish Gaelic

classes, immersion programs, community events, and promotional activities for people of all ages.

Ireland's Great Hunger Institute and Museum
Quinnipiac University
275 Mount Carmel Avenue
Hamden, CT 06518
(203) 582-4564
Website: https://www.qu.edu/on-campus/institutes-centers
/irelands-great-hunger-institute.html
This academic institute is devoted to scholarship about the Great Famine and its impact on Ireland and Irish Americans. It has an extensive collection of primary sources, including nineteenth-century political cartoons, and it runs exhibits at its accompanying museum.

Irish Association of Manitoba (IAM)
654 Erin Street
Winnipeg, Manitoba R3G 2V9
Canada
(204) 772-8830
Website: http://irishassociation.ca
The IAM supports Irish theater, choir, and other group-oriented festivities that contribute to cultural development.

Irish International Immigrant Center (IIIC)
One State Street, Suite 800
Boston, MA 02109

(617) 542-7654
Website: http://www.iiicenter.org
Facebook: @IIICenter
Twitter: @iiicenter
The IIIC assists recent immigrants from various countries
  with their legal needs and their health and case-
  management needs. It also provides social opportunities
  and Irish-language classes. The center also has career
  classes, US citizenship instruction, and mentorship.

Irish Lobby for Immigration Reform
875 6th Avenue, Suite 201
New York, NY 10001
(917) 251-0739
Website: http://irishlobbyusa.org
Facebook: @IrishLobbyForImmigrationReform
Twitter: @ILIR_Tweets
The Irish Lobby for Immigration Reform was established in
  2005 to create a volunteer-based political action lobby to
  petition American legislators to enable Irish immigration
  and to help Irish immigrants in other ways.

Library and Archives Canada
395 Wellington Street
Ottawa, ON K1A 0N4
Canada
(866) 578-7777
Website: http://www.collectionscanada.ca/ireland

/index-e.html
Facebook: @LibraryArchives
Twitter: @LibraryArchives
This organization holds records of Irish immigrants, including
passenger lists and resources for tracking down people of
Irish ancestry for those working on genealogy.

NYC St. Patrick's Day Parade
PO Box 295, Woodlawn Station
Bronx, NY 10470
(718) 231-4400
Website: https://www.nycstpatricksparade.org
Facebook: @NYCStPatricksDayParade
Twitter: @StPatsParadeNYC
The New York City St. Patrick's Day Parade has marched
through New York City since 1762. The Fighting
Sixty-Ninth Regiment leads the march of 150,000
participants as 2 million spectators watch. Other military
organizations, pipe bands, Ancient Order of Hibernians
groups, political organizations, Irish County associations,
and other groups march in it.

FOR FURTHER READING

Cook, Peter. *You Wouldn't Want to Sail the Seas!* San Diego, CA: Parfait Press, 2012.

Daly, Ita. *Stories from Ireland.* Oxford, UK: Oxford University Press, 2013.

Fitzpatrick, Marie-Louise. *The Long March: The Choctaw's Gift to Irish Famine Relief.* Columbus, OH: Zaner-Bloser, 2013.

Ganeri, Anita. *Republic of Ireland.* Chicago, IL: Heinemann Raintree, 2015.

Lenihan, Edmund, and Alan Clarke. *Irish Tales of Mystery and Magic.* Cork, Ireland: Mercier Press, 2015.

Murray, Julie. *Saint Patrick's Day.* Edina, MN: ABDO, 2012.

Sherman, Jill. *The Irish Potato Famine: A Cause-and-Effect Investigation.* Minneapolis, MN: Lerner Publications, 2017.

Swain, Gwenyth. *Hope and Tears: Ellis Island Voices.* Honesdale, PA: Calkins Creek, 2012.

Thomas, Zachary, and Natashya Wilson. *The Melting Pot: The People and Cultures of New York.* New York: Rosen Classroom, 2012.

Wallenfeldt, Jeffrey H. *Ireland.* New York: Britannica Educational Publishing in association with Rosen Educational Services, 2014.

Bardon, Jonathan. *A History of Ulster*. Belfast, UK: The Blackstaff Press, 1997.

Beeman, Richard R. *The Evolution of the Southern Backcountry: A Case Study of Lunenburg County, Virginia, 1746–1832*. Philadelphia, PA: University of Pennsylvania Press, 1984.

Blackwell, Amy Hackney, and Ryan Hackney. *The Everything Irish History & Heritage Book: From Brian Boru and St. Patrick to Sinn Fein and the Troubles, All You Need to Know About the Emerald Isle*. Avon, MA: Adams Media, 2004.

Crozier, Alan. "The Scotch-Irish Influence on American English." American Speech 59, no. 4 (1984). doi:10.2307/454783.

Cusack, Margaret Anna. *The Nun of Kenmare*. Cork, Ireland: Mercier Press, 1970.

Dezell, Maureen. *Irish America: Coming Into Clover: The Evolution of a People and a Culture*. New York: Doubleday, 2001.

Goddard, Sean. "Hoedowns, Reels, and Frolics: Roots and Branches of Southern Appalachian Dance." *Folk Music Journal* 11 no. 2 (2017).

Griffin, William D. *The Book of Irish Americans*. New York: Times Books, 1990.

Josefiak, Melissa. "'The Woman Came To Do Laundry…': Depression-Era Domestic Servants in Greater Hartford, Connecticut." Wethersfield Historical Society, August 8, 2012. http://wethersfieldhistory.org/articles-from-the -community/the_woman_came_to_do_laundry.

Kelly, Mary C. *The Shamrock and the Lily: The New York Irish and the Creation of a Transatlantic Identity, 1845–1921.* New York: Peter Lang, 2005.

Kenny, Kevin. *The American Irish: A History.* New York: Routledge, 2016.

Langrall, Peggy. "Appalachian Folk Music: From Foothills to Footlights." *Music Educators Journal* 72, no. 7 (March 1986).

Lee, Joseph, and Marion R. Casey. *Making the Irish American: History and Heritage of the Irish in the United States.* New York: New York University Press, 2007.

Leyburn, James Graham. *The Scotch-Irish: A Social History.* Chapel Hill, NC: University of North Carolina Press, 1989.

Nicholson, Asenath. *Annals of the Famine in Ireland in 1847, 1848, and 1849.* Kessinger Legacy Reprints, 2015.

O'Grada, Cormac. *The Great Irish Famine.* Cambridge, UK: Cambridge University Press, 2000.

Straw, Richard A., and H. Tyler Blethen, eds. *High Mountains Rising: Appalachia in Time and Place.* Champaign, IL: University of Illinois Press, 2004.

ABOUT THE AUTHOR

Dr. Sean Heather K. McGraw is an adjunct lecturer at Marist College and a former adjunct lecturer at various institutions, including SUNY Albany and Siena College. She has also been a librarian and national park guide. She is writing a book called *The Land and Hearth: Margaret Anna Cusack, Defender of Irish Girls.* Other work has been published by Rosen Publishing. She is also a harpist, storyteller, and amateur actor.

PHOTO CREDITS